READING FUNDAMENTALS

by Aileen Weintraub

GRADE
1

New York

New York

An Imprint of Sterling Publishing
1166 Avenue of the Americas
New York, NY 10036

ISBN 978-1-4114-7199-3

Distributed in Canada by Sterling Publishing
C/o Canadian Manda Group, 664 Annette Street
Toronto, Ontario, Canada M6S 2C8
Distributed in the United Kingdom by GMC Distribution Services
Castle Place, 166 High Street, Lewes, East Sussex, England BN7 1XU
Distributed in Australia by Capricorn Link (Australia) Pty. Ltd.
P.O. Box 704, Windsor, NSW 2756, Australia

For information about custom editions, special sales, and premium and corporate purchases, please contact Sterling Special Sales at 800-805-5489 or specialsales@sterlingpublishing.com.

Manufactured in Canada
Lot #:
2 4 6 8 10 9 7 5 3
02/16

www.flashkids.com

Dear Parent,

Being able to read and understand nonfiction texts is an essential skill that not only ensures success in the classroom, but also in college and beyond. Why is nonfiction reading important? For one thing, close reading of nonfiction texts helps build critical thinking skills. Another reason nonfiction reading is important is that it builds your child's background knowledge. That means your child will already have a wealth of knowledge about various subjects to build on as he or she progresses in school. You can feel good knowing you'll be laying the foundation for future success by ensuring that your child develops the necessary skills that nonfiction reading comprehension provides.

The activities in this workbook are meant for your child to be able to do on his or her own. However, you can assist your child with difficult words, ideas, and questions. Reading comprehension skills take time to develop, so patience is important. After your child has completed each activity, you can go over the answers together using the answer key provided in the back of this workbook. Provide encouragement and a sense of accomplishment to your child as you go along!

Extending reading comprehension beyond this workbook is beneficial and provides your child with the opportunity to see why this skill is so essential. You might read a newspaper article together and then discuss the main ideas, or head to the library to find a book on your child's favorite subject. Remember, reading is fun. It opens the door to imagination!

Make a Berry Smoothie!

Smoothies are yummy! They are cool on a hot day.
They are healthy too. Ask a grown-up to help you.

You will need:

1 ½ cups mixed berries

1 cup ice

1 cup milk

1 teaspoon honey

Put it all in a blender. Mix until smooth.
Pour into a glass. Enjoy!

Answer the questions below.

1. What kind of berries will you need?

_____

2. How much milk will you need?

_____

3. How much honey will you need?

_____

4. What will you use to mix the smoothie?

_____

Red Light, Green Light

Do you like to play games? Red Light, Green Light is a fun game. Kids line up in a row. The teacher stands in front. The teacher calls out "green light"! The kids run toward the teacher. The teacher calls out "red light"! The kids stop. The teacher calls out "green light"! The kids run again. The first one to reach the teacher wins!

Answer the questions below.

1. Where does the teacher stand?

_____

2. When do the kids go?

_____

3. When do the kids stop?

_____

4. How does someone win?

_____

Let's Play Hot Potato

Have you played Hot Potato? This game will make you giggle. Sit in a circle on the floor or grass with your friends. Ask a grown-up to turn on music. Then, pass a bean bag around the circle. The bean bag is the hot potato. Pass it quickly! Soon the adult will turn the music off. The kid still holding the bean bag is out. Play again. The last kid in the circle is the winner!

Circle the correct answers below.

1. What do you pass around the circle?

2. To start, what must you do?   sit   stand   dance

3. What does a grown-up turn on?   a toaster   a buzzer   music

4. Who is the winner?

   the first kid in the circle   the last kid in the circle   the adult

The US Constitution

The United States used to be part of England. The people of the United States fought to be free. After the Revolutionary War they needed a plan. In 1787, a group of men wrote new laws. They called it the Constitution. All the people had to follow these laws. This helped to make sure people lived in peace. Today the US Constitution is the oldest in the world. The laws of the Constitution are still followed.

What is the order? Draw a line to each step.

First	A group of men wrote new laws.
Second	The laws of the Constitution are still followed.
Third	The US was part of England.
Fourth	They fought to be free.

Looking at a Map

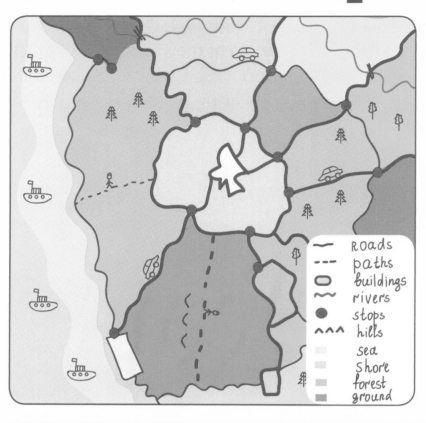

roads
paths
buildings
rivers
stops
hills
sea
shore
forest
ground

Have you ever looked at a map? Maps are small pictures of bigger places. They tell us where things are. Maps have symbols. A symbol is a picture. These pictures help us find what we are looking for. Maps also have a key. This is not the same as a door key. A map key is usually in the corner of the map. It tells what the symbols mean.

Answer the questions below.

1. What does a map tell us?

_____

2. What are two things a map has?

_____

3. What is a symbol?

_____

4. Where do you usually find a map key on a map?

_____

Fall Fun!

Fall is a nice time of year. It is sunny during the day. The weather gets cooler. The leaves change colors. Soon they will fall from the trees. Animals prepare for winter. They stock up on food. Birds begin to look for warmer weather. You can carve pumpkins. Many people go apple picking. They can make apple cider or even apple pie. Yum!

Complete the sentences.

1. In fall, the leaves change _____ .

2. Soon the leaves will _____ from the trees.

3. Animals begin to stock up on _____ .

4. Birds begin to look for _____ weather.

Globes!

Have you ever used a globe? A globe is a model of Earth. Earth is very big. You can see the whole world on a globe. A globe shows us land and water. The big areas of land are called continents. The big areas of water are the oceans. There are seven continents. There are five oceans. Can you find them on a globe?

Circle the correct answers below.

1. What is a globe?	a model	an animal	a book
2. What are continents?	land	chairs	houses
3. What are the big areas of water called?	parks	oceans	school
4. How many oceans are there?	two	five	six

All about Mottos

A motto is a saying. Every state has a motto. The motto is on many state seals. Sometimes it is on a state flag. The United States has a motto too. The motto for the United States is "In God We Trust." Do you have a coin? Look at it. What do you see? Can you see the motto? You can also find the motto on paper money.

Circle the correct answers below.

1. What is a motto?   a saying   a song   a dance

2. Where is a place you
   can find a state motto?   a pen   a peanut   a state seal

3. What is the motto for the United States?

   Be Prepared   In God We Trust   Do No Harm

4. Where can you find the US motto?

Traffic Safety

Do you like to go for walks? Walks can be fun. It's important to follow traffic rules. Always walk on the sidewalk or on a path. Before crossing the street, make sure you are with an adult. Be sure to stand at the crosswalk. Wait for the Walk sign. Look both ways. Have all the cars stopped? When you are sure it is safe, you can cross. Enjoy your walk!

What is the order? Draw a line to each step.

First	Look both ways.
Second	Stand at the crosswalk.
Third	Cross the street.
Fourth	Wait for the Walk sign.

Bikes Are Cool!

Riding a bike is a good way to travel. You can visit friends or go to the park. Safety comes first. Make sure you have a helmet that fits. Do you know the traffic signs? You might want to go over them. Cross at the corner. Walk your bike across the street. It is also a good idea to wear bright-colored clothing. This way others can easily see you. Now you are ready to roll.

Circle **yes** or **no**.

1. Always wear a helmet.	Yes	No
2. Cross in the middle of the street.	Yes	No
3. Wear bright-colored clothing.	Yes	No
4. Always walk your bike across the street.	Yes	No

Collecting Seashells

Summer is the hottest time of year. It is a good time to go to the beach. You can gather seashells. You can swim. The best time to explore is at low tide. You can see the treasures the ocean has left behind. Shells are made by small animals. They used to live in them. Shells come in all shapes and sizes. Wash them out and take them home!

Answer the questions below.

1. When is the hottest time of the year?

   _____

2. What is something you can do at the beach?

   _____

3. What is the best time of day to look for seashells?

   _____

4. What makes seashells?

   _____

Travel, Then and Now

There are many ways to travel. You can ride in a car. You can take a train. You can fly in a plane. But this wasn't always possible. Long ago, people used to travel with the help of animals. They rode in carriages pulled by horses. It took a lot longer to get places. It could take months to go across the country. Now we can cross it in a day!

Circle the correct answers below.

1. How many ways are there to travel?

    one   many   none

2. What did people ride in long ago?

    carriages   boxes   houses

3. What did people use to help them travel?

4. How long did it used to take to travel across the country?

    days   hours   months

Feeding Your Brain

Your brain is always working. It has a hard job. It runs your whole body. It helps you think. It helps you remember. It helps you blink. It is even in charge of your dreams. It is important to keep your brain healthy. You can do this by eating right. Exercise is also good for your brain. You can make your brain stronger by reading and doing puzzles. These are all ways to feed your brain.

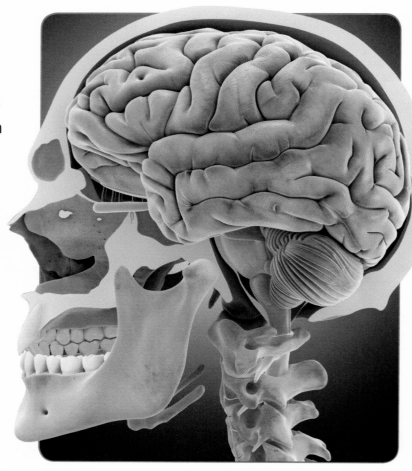

Complete the sentences. Use the words shown.

dreams   body   puzzles   eating

1. Your brain runs your whole _____ .

2. Your brain is in charge of your _____ .

3. You can keep your brain healthy by _____ right.

4. You can make your brain stronger by reading and doing _____ .

Recycle!

Earth is very special to us. That is why we must care for it. One way is to recycle. *Recycle* means "to use again." Glass, metal, and plastic can be recycled. Cardboard and paper can also be recycled. Recycling goes in special bins. These bins are picked up and taken away. They go to a place that sorts the trash. Then the trash is cleaned. It is also processed. It is ready to be used for something new!

What is the order? Draw a line to each step.

First	Trash is cleaned.
Second	People put their trash in special bins.
Third	The trash is ready to be used for something new.
Fourth	The bins are picked up.

Our First President

George Washington was the first president of the United States. He grew up in Virginia. George lived on a farm with his family. Later, he joined the army. He helped win a big war. Then he became president. George had a lot of work to do. The states were fighting over land. He wanted to fix things. He helped make new laws. We still follow a lot of these laws today.

Circle yes or no.

1. George Washington was the second president of the United States.	Yes	No
2. George Washington lived on a farm with his family.	Yes	No
3. George Washington was never in the army.	Yes	No
4. George Washington helped win a big war.	Yes	No

Our Sun

The sun is high in the sky. It is very bright. It is not solid like Earth. Instead, it is made up of gas. The sun has an important job. We could not live without it. The sun keeps us warm. It also gives us light. This light helps grow food such as plants. We would not have food without the sun. Sunlight is reflected by the moon. This makes the moon shine bright.

Circle the correct answers below.

1. What is the sun made of?   rock   gas   flowers

2. What does the sun give us?   darkness   light   rest

3. What does the sun help us grow?

4. What does the moon reflect?   sunlight   Earth   grass

Feel the Beat

Put your hand on your chest. Can you feel your heartbeat? Your heart is a big muscle. It is the size of your fist. Sometimes your heart beats fast. This happens when you are excited. It can happen when you are scared too. When you are relaxed, your heartbeat slows. Your heart is like a pump. It pumps blood to your body. When your heart beats faster you are pumping more blood. Blood goes to your muscles. It also goes to your brain.

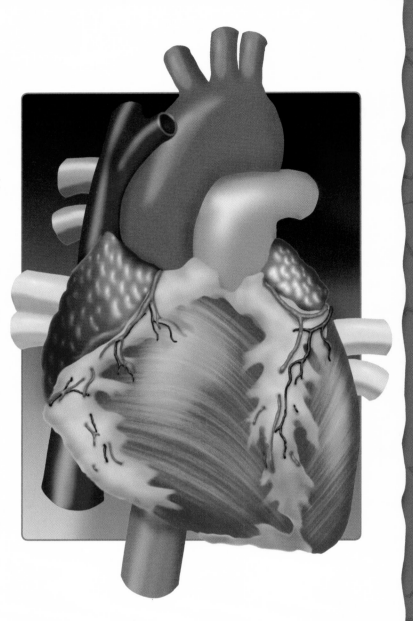

Circle **yes** or **no**.

1. Your heart is a big muscle.	Yes	No
2. Your heart is the size of your head.	Yes	No
3. Your heart pumps blood to your body.	Yes	No
4. Your heart beats faster when you are resting.	Yes	No

Pizza Bagels

Bagels taste good! Pizza tastes good! Let's make pizza bagels! Make sure a grown-up helps you.

You will need:
One bagel
Tomato sauce
Shredded cheese
Toppings

Ask a grown-up to set the oven to 375°F (190°C). Cut the bagel in half. Spread tomato sauce on the bagel. Put on the cheese. Add the toppings. Bake the bagel on a baking sheet for 5–8 minutes. Let it cool. Now it's ready to eat!

What is the order? Draw a line to each step.

First	Add the toppings.
Second	Bake the bagel.
Third	Cut the bagel in half.
Fourth	Put on the tomato sauce and cheese.

All About Blubber

Whales swim deep in the ocean. They swim underwater. It is dark. There is very little sunlight. It can get very cold. But whales have a way of keeping warm. They have blubber! Blubber is a layer of fat. It acts like a warm blanket. Whales need to build up their blubber. They do this by eating a lot in warm weather. The blubber gives them energy for the long winters.

Complete the sentences. Use the words shown.

sunlight	blanket	warm	fat

1. There is very little _____ underwater.

2. Whales have a way of keeping _____ .

3. Blubber is a layer of _____ .

4. Blubber acts like a warm _____ .

Winter!

Winter is cold. It is the coldest season of the year. The days are short. The nights are long. Most trees and flowers do not grow. Some animals hibernate, or sleep, all winter. In some places it snows. The snow stays on the ground for a long time. This is because it is too cold for it to melt. When snow melts it can refreeze. This is how icicles are formed. Brrr! Don't forget to dress warm!

Circle **yes** or **no**.

1. Winter is the coldest season of the year.	Yes	No
2. Most trees and flowers grow a lot in winter.	Yes	No
3. Some animals hibernate, or sleep, in winter.	Yes	No
4. Snow can never refreeze.	Yes	No

Falling Leaves

Leaves come in many shapes and sizes. They can have a zigzag shape. They may be round and smooth. Leaves are green in the spring and summer. The green color helps the leaves make food and water. In the fall, it is cold. It is too cold to make food. The leaves dry out. They change color. They turn red, yellow, orange, and brown. Then they begin to fall from the trees. New leaves will grow again in spring.

What is the order? Draw a line to each step.

First   The leaves change color.

Second   It is too cold to make food.

Third   The leaves fall from the trees.

Fourth   The leaves dry out.

Going to the Library

Do you like to go to the library? The library is a great place. You can check out books for free. There are a few ways to find books there. Did you know storybooks are in alphabetical order? Look for the author's last name. Don't worry if you don't know it. You can look on the computer. Just search for the name of the book. You can also ask a librarian.

Complete the sentences. Use the words shown.

name	free	librarian	computer

1. At the library, you can check out books for _____ .

2. To find a book, you look for the author's last _____ .

3. You can also look on the _____ .

4. If you have any questions, you can ask a _____ .

A Great Inventor

Thomas Edison was a great inventor. He was born in Ohio in 1847. Thomas was always coming up with new ideas. He set up his first lab in his parents' house. He was young. He was only 10. Later, he invented the phonograph. He was able to record sound. He also invented the first light bulb. He even helped invent the first movies! He had over 1,000 inventions. We still use some of his inventions today.

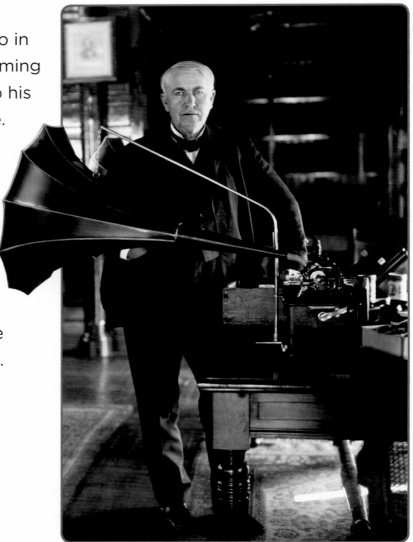

Circle yes or no.

1. Thomas Edison was an inventor.	Yes	No
2. He set up his first lab in his barn.	Yes	No
3. The phonograph recorded movies.	Yes	No
4. He invented cars.	Yes	No

What Happens When You Blink?

Do you blink when dust gets in your eyes? You do! Most people don't think about blinking. It just happens. Blinking helps protect our eyes. Blinking keeps our eyes from getting dry. It also keeps out dirt. Our eyelids are like dust catchers. Most people blink 15 times in one minute. That's a lot of blinking!

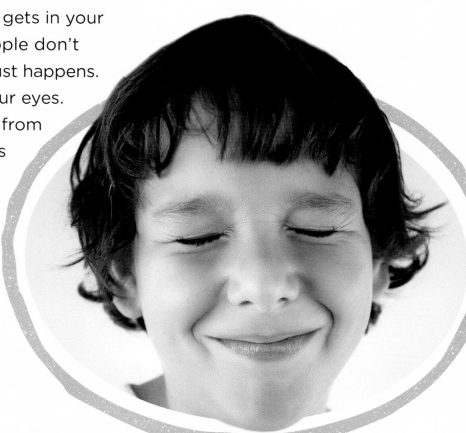

Circle the correct answers below.

1. What does blinking protect?

2. What does blinking keep our eyes from getting? happy wet dry

3. What does blinking keep out of our eyes? dirt tears birds

4. How many times per minute do we blink? one 15 five

27

All About Bats

Bats are mammals. They are the only mammals that can fly. A bat's body is covered in fur. Its wings are smooth. A bat's wings feel like leather. Bats like to sleep during the daytime. They sleep upside down! They look for food at night. Most like to eat bugs or fruit. There are many kinds of bats. Bats can be found all over the world.

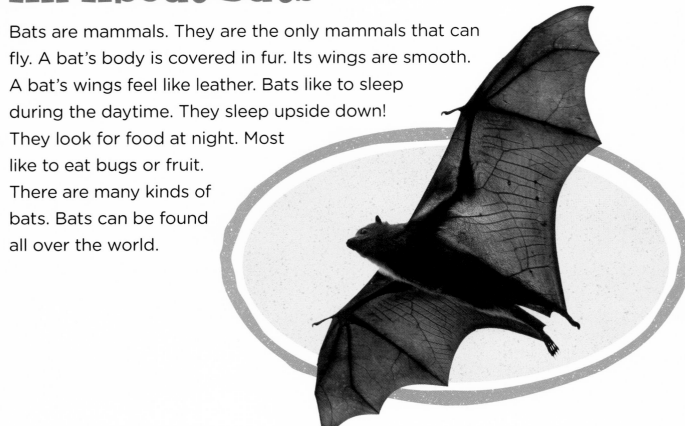

Answer the questions below.

1. What is a bat's body covered in?

_____

2. What do a bat's wings feel like?

_____

3. When do bats sleep?

_____

4. What do bats like to eat?

_____

Hibernation

It is not easy for animals to live outside in winter. It gets very cold. There is little food to be found. Some animals hibernate. This means they go to sleep for the whole winter. First, they eat a lot of food. Then they find a warm shelter. Here they go to sleep. They can sleep for six months. Their heartbeat slows down. Their temperature drops. When they wake up it is spring. They are very hungry.

What is the order? Draw a line to each step.

First	They find a warm shelter.
Second	They go to sleep.
Third	They wake up to spring.
Fourth	Animals eat a lot of food.

Drinking Water

All living things need water. This includes you! Drinking water is good for you. Water makes up half your body. It is in your blood. It helps you digest food. You even need water to sweat. It is a good idea to drink water when you are thirsty. You can eat fruit too. It has a lot of water in it! Drink more when it is hot outside. Without water you can get sick. No one can live without water.

Circle the correct answers below.

1. What do all living things need?   tea   ice cream   water

2. What part of your body has water?   bones   blood   toenails

3. What food has a lot of water in it?

4. How much of your body does water make up?   half   all   none

Yawn!

Do you ever yawn? Do you know that animals yawn too? We yawn when we are tired. We might yawn when we are bored. Some people yawn when they are feeling stressed. No one is sure why. It might mean we need more air. Some scientists say that yawning helps wake us up. One thing is for sure: Yawning can be catching. Notice the next time you yawn. Did the person next to you yawn too?

Complete the sentences. Use the words shown.

catching	tired	wake	why

1. We yawn when we are _____ .

2. Scientists don't know _____ we yawn.

3. Yawning may help _____ us up.

4. Yawning can be _____ .

Two Ears Are Better Than One

Ears are for hearing. We have two ears. Having two ears helps you know where sound is coming from. First, sound enters your ear. Then a part of your ear sends a message to your brain. Your brain tells you what the sound is. Sounds from the right go to your right ear first. Sounds from the left go to your left ear first. What if a sound is right behind you? It will go to both ears at the same time!

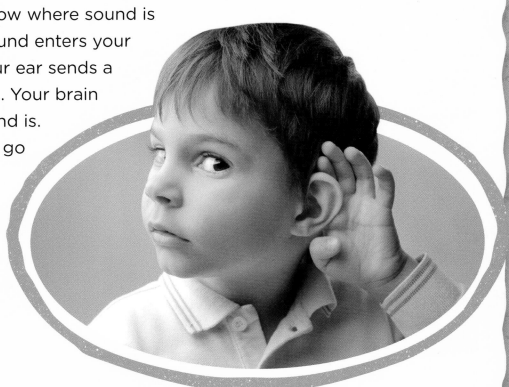

Answer the questions below.

1. What is the main idea of this text?

   _____

2. How do you know what sound you're hearing?

   _____

3. How do you hear sounds from your right side?

   _____

4. How do you hear sounds from behind you?

   _____

Making Energy

Your body needs energy. Energy helps keep you alive. Your body gets energy from healthy food. Some healthy foods are fruits and vegetables. Exercise also gives you energy. It makes your muscles strong. It helps you breathe better. Exercise helps build stronger bones. There are many ways to get exercise. You can play outside. You can run. You can dance. When you exercise you feel better. You have more energy to play.

Circle **yes** or **no**.

1. Energy helps keep you alive.	Yes	No
2. Fruits and vegetables are not healthy.	Yes	No
3. Exercise makes your muscles strong.	Yes	No
4. Exercise will not help build stronger bones.	Yes	No

The American Flag

The American flag has a nickname. It is called Old Glory. Many people think that Betsy Ross made the first flag. The first flag had 13 stars and 13 stripes. That has changed. Now it has 50 stars. It still has 13 stripes. The stars are for the 50 states. The stripes are for the first colonies. There are many songs and poems about the American flag. Do you know any?

Answer the questions below.

1. What is the flag's nickname?

_____

2. Who do people think made the first flag?

_____

3. How many stars did the first flag have?

_____

4. How many stripes does the flag have now?

_____

Harriet Tubman

Harriet Tubman was born a slave. She lived in a one-room cabin with her family. She had a hard life. She eventually ran away. She was free from slavery. She wanted to help others. She led many slaves to freedom. She helped them hide. She also helped them stay safe. This was done in secret because it was very dangerous work. Harriet Tubman was very brave.

Fill in the blanks.

1. Harriet Tubman was born a _____ .

2. She lived with her _____ .

3. She led many slaves to _____ .

4. Her work was done in _____ .

A Tree Grows

Trees grow in many ways. Roots grow down. They grow deep down into the earth. Branches grow up. They stretch high in the sky. Trees grow wider and taller. They even grow rings inside their trunks. Every ring means one year of growth. This is how we tell the age of a tree. When you see a tree stump, find the rings. Count them. You will know how old the tree was when it was cut down.

Answer the questions below.

1. Where do tree roots grow?

_____

2. Where do the branches stretch to?

_____

3. What do trees grow inside their trunk?

_____

4. What does every ring stand for?

_____

Life Cycle of a Chicken

Chickens are birds. These birds live on farms. A hen is a female chicken. A pullet is a young hen. When a pullet is six months old, she starts laying eggs. Then she sits on her eggs. This keeps them warm. Soon they will hatch. Baby chicks peck their way out. They will look for food. They eat insects and worms. Baby chicks will grow into hens and roosters. They can live for up to 15 years.

What is the order? Draw a line to each step.

First	Baby chicks peck their way out.
Second	Baby chicks look for food.
Third	A hen is ready to lay eggs.
Fourth	The hen sits on her eggs.

Mount Rushmore

Have you heard of Mount Rushmore? Mount Rushmore is a mountain. This mountain has giant faces on it! It took 14 years to build. Workers blasted rocks to make the faces. They are the faces of four US presidents. These presidents helped form the country. Mount Rushmore honors these presidents. It is a symbol of hope and freedom. You can go to Mount Rushmore. It is in South Dakota.

Complete the sentences.

1. Mount Rushmore has _____ on it.

2. They are the faces of four US _____ .

3. These presidents helped form our _____ .

4. Mount Rushmore is a symbol of _____ and _____ .

Make a Terrarium

A terrarium is a small garden. To make a terrarium, you will need:

- A glass jar
- Pebbles
- Activated charcoal
- Soil
- Small plants

Cover the bottom of the jar with pebbles.

Add a layer of charcoal.

Fill the jar halfway with soil.

Plant the plants.

Water the plants.

You can add rocks and pine cones.

Put the jar in a sunny place.

Water your plants when the soil is dry.

What is the order? Draw a line to each step.

First	Water the plants.
Second	Plant the plants.
Third	Cover the bottom of the jar with pebbles.
Fourth	Fill the jar halfway with soil.

Comparing with a Venn Diagram

Venn diagrams are useful. They help us compare and contrast. Venn diagrams use two circles. The circles overlap. Look at the diagram below. There are three parts. The left side has facts about cats. The right side has facts about dogs. The middle has an area that's part of both circles. In this area, there are facts about both and cats and dogs.

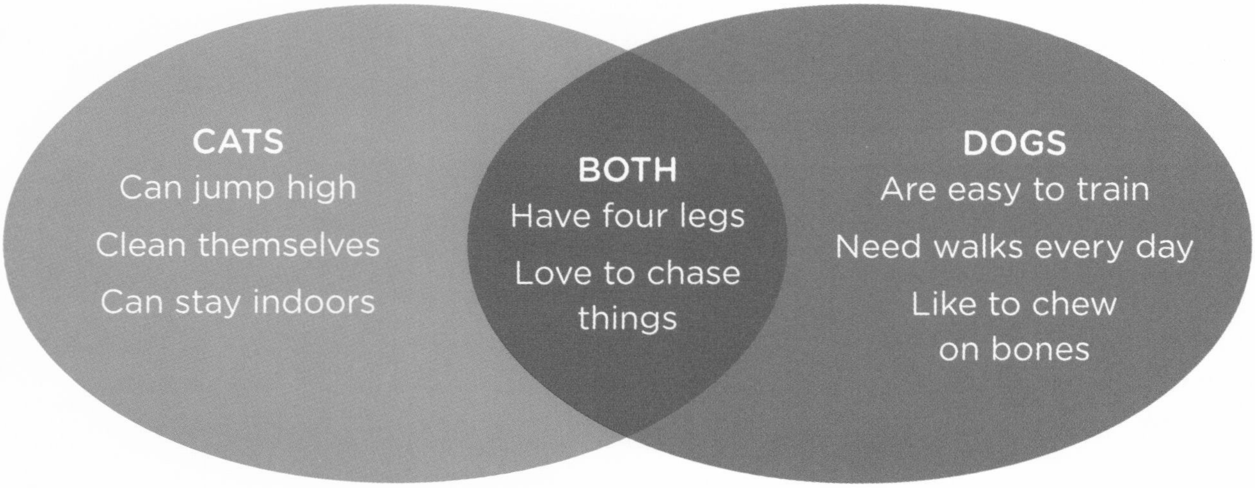

CATS
Can jump high

Clean themselves

Can stay indoors

BOTH
Have four legs

Love to chase things

DOGS
Are easy to train

Need walks every day

Like to chew on bones

Answer the questions below.

1. Which animal needs to be walked?

_____

2. Which animal cleans itself?

_____

3. What does the list in the middle of Venn diagram show?

_____

4. What does a Venn diagram do?

_____

Benjamin Franklin

Benjamin Franklin was a Founding Father. He was also an inventor. He was born in Boston more than 300 years ago. Ben quit school when he was 10 years old. He went to work when he was 12. He spent a lot of time reading books. This made him smart. When he grew up he had many interests. He helped pass laws. He experimented with electricity. Later, he helped start a library. There is a picture of him on the US $100 bill.

Circle the correct answers below.

1. Where was Benjamin Franklin born?	Boston	New York	Ohio
2. How old was he when he quit school?	10	12	9
3. What did Benjamin Franklin help pass?	boats	laws	apples

4. What did he experiment with?

Moving Clouds

Look at the sky. Do you see clouds? Watch them for a while. Clouds are always moving. They change shape and size. They are made of tiny drops of water. Dark clouds can mean rain is on the way. Fluffy clouds come out on sunny days. Sometimes clouds look like other things. What do the clouds look like to you? You can make this into a game with your friends.

Complete the sentences.

1. Clouds are always _____ .

2. Clouds are made of tiny drops of _____ .

3. Dark clouds mean _____ .

4. Fluffy clouds come out on _____ days.

All About Snails

Snails have soft bodies. They have hard shells. They like damp places. Snails hide in the daytime. Sometimes they hide under rocks. They come out at night to eat. Snails eat soft shoots and leaves. Next time you see a snail, watch it move. It will leave behind a trail of slime. The slime protects the snail's foot. It acts like padding. It also helps it hold on as it moves.

Answer the questions below.

1. What kind of places do snails like?

_____

2. When do they come out to eat?

_____

3. What does a snail leave behind when it moves?

_____

4. What does the slime do for the snails when they move?

_____

Looking for Rainbows

Have you ever seen a rainbow? You can see one after it rains. The sun comes out. It shines between the clouds. It beams through drops of water. That's when you can see a rainbow! The colors of a rainbow are red, orange, yellow, green, blue, indigo, and violet. They are always the same order. Red is on top. Violet is on the bottom. Next time it rains, look up in the sky. You might see a rainbow!

Circle **yes** or **no**.

1. The sun shines through drops of water to make a rainbow.	Yes	No
2. The colors of the rainbow are always in the same order.	Yes	No
3. Green is always on top.	Yes	No
4. Yellow is always on the bottom.	Yes	No

A Gift of Freedom

The Statue of Liberty is a symbol of freedom. It was a gift from France. The French wanted to show their friendship. The trip from France was hard. The statue had to be shipped in pieces. It was stored in many crates. Then it sailed on a ship. The ship took it across the ocean. The statue had to be put together. That took four months. It was placed in New York Harbor. There, workers put it together. If you go to New York City, you can visit it!

What is the order? Draw a line to each step.

First	It was placed in New York Harbor.
Second	The French wanted to show their friendship.
Third	It had to be put together.
Fourth	The statue was shipped in pieces.

Tadpoles

Frogs lay eggs in spring. They lay their eggs in ponds. The eggs hatch after 10 days. Baby frogs are called tadpoles. Tadpoles swim out of the eggs. They are hungry. They swim around. They look for food. They don't look like frogs at all. Soon they will grow legs. Then they will come up for air. By the time they are 12 weeks old, they have turned into tiny frogs. They are ready to be on land.

Answer the questions below.

1. When do frogs lay eggs?

_____

2. How long does it take for frog eggs to hatch?

_____

3. What are baby frogs called?

_____

4. Name three things that tadpoles do:

_____

_____

From Caterpillar to Butterfly

A butterfly lays eggs on a leaf. Soon a caterpillar hatches. It lives on leaves. It loves to eat. It eats and eats. It grows bigger and bigger. Then the caterpillar makes a hard case to wrap around itself. This case is called a pupa. The caterpillar stays in the pupa. Slowly it turns into a butterfly. The pupa breaks open. A beautiful butterfly flies out.

Answer the questions below.

1. Where does a butterfly lay its eggs?

_____

2. What do caterpillars love to do?

_____

3. What is the hard case a caterpillar wraps itself in called?

_____

4. What happens when the pupa breaks open?

_____

Spring!

In the spring, the weather gets warmer. Roots and shoots begin to grow. Many people plant a garden. The sun stays out longer. It warms the earth. Spring showers water the soil. This helps flowers bloom. It also helps vegetables grow. Birds build their nests. They lay their eggs in spring. New babies hatch. These babies learn to find food in the warm weather. When winter comes, they are big and strong.

Complete the sentences.

1. In the spring, the weather gets _____ .

2. Roots and shoots begin to _____ .

3. The sun stays out longer and warms the _____ .

4. Birds build their _____ .

Buckle Up!

Riding in a car can be fun. What is the first thing you do when you get in the car? Do you buckle up? Using a seatbelt keeps you safe. It is an important rule. Everyone in the car needs to buckle up. This means the grown-ups too! In most states, wearing a seatbelt is the law. It doesn't matter if you are going on a short trip or a long one. Don't forget to buckle up. Enjoy the ride!

Circle **yes** or **no**.

1. Grown-ups should wear seatbelts.	Yes	No
2. Wearing a seatbelt is important.	Yes	No
3. You only have to buckle up for long trips.	Yes	No
4. Seatbelts don't keep you safe.	Yes	No

Make a Shadow Clock

In summer, the sun rises high in the sky. It is a good time to make a shadow clock. Go outside on a sunny morning. Stand with your feet together. Give a friend a piece of chalk. Ask your friend to draw an outline around your shadow with chalk. Then color in the outline. Write down the time. Do this again every two hours. You will see how your shadow moves. Now you have a shadow clock.

What is the order? Draw a line to each step.

First	Write down the time.
Second	Stand with your feet together.
Third	Go outside on a sunny morning.
Fourth	Ask a friend to draw an outline around your shadow.
Fifth	Color in the outline with chalk.

Insects!

Turn over a stone. Dig up some dirt from the ground. This is a good way to hunt for insects. You can find many kinds of insects. They live in fields and woods. They also live in streams. Some insects lay eggs in the soil. Baby bugs hatch from the eggs. They are called grubs and larvae. They can live in the soil for a long time. They eat the roots of plants. Soon they will change and grow. Then they go above the ground.

Circle the correct answers below.

1. Where is a place insects live?

2. Where do some insects lay their eggs?   soil   chairs   tables

3. What is one name for a baby insect?   chick   fawn   grub

4. What do some insects eat?   roots   tin cans   plastic

Declaration of Independence

In 1776, America was at war. The first settlers were fighting the British. The first settlers were called colonists. The British ruled the colonists. The colonists wanted to be free. The colonists won the war. New leaders wrote the Declaration of Independence. It said that all men were equal. The Declaration of Independence was signed on the Fourth of July. Now the colonies could make their own rules. You can still see the Declaration of Independence. It is in Washington, DC.

Answer the questions.

1. Whom were the colonists fighting?

_____

2. Who won the war?

_____

3. What did the Declaration of Independence say all men were?

_____

4. What could the colonies now make on their own?

_____

The President's House

Have you ever wondered where the president lives? He lives in the White House! The White House is in Washington, DC. It is a big, white house. It has 132 rooms. Some are just for the president's family. Others are for meetings. You can visit some of these rooms. It would be fun to see what this house looks like. When a new president moves in, the old one moves out.

Circle the correct answers below.

1. Who lives in the White House?	president	soldiers	circus
2. Where is the White House?	Washington, DC	Boston	New York
3. How many rooms are in the White House?	100	13	132
4. What are some of the rooms for?	games	swimming	meetings

Summer!

In summer, it is hot. The days are longer than any other time. The nights are short. People spend a lot of time outdoors during summer. It's a great time to work in the garden. It is also a great time for swimming. Some people like to barbecue. Many fruits and vegetables grow in summer. Best of all, children are on vacation!

Complete the sentences.

1. The temperature in summer is _____ .

2. The days are _____ in summer.

3. People spend a lot of time _____ .

4. Many fruits and vegetables _____ in summer.

A Compass Rose

A compass rose is a symbol found on maps. It can help you find your way. It is called a rose because it looks like a flower. It helps with directions. It shows you north, south, east, and west. It also shows you northeast, northwest, southeast, and southwest. North is on the top. South is on the bottom. West is to the left. East is to the right.

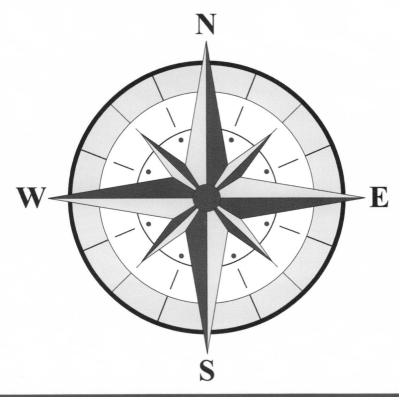

Answer the questions below. Use the words shown.

up	down	left	right

1. On a map, north is _____ .

2. On a map, south is _____ .

3. On a map, west is _____ .

4. On a map, east is _____ .

Getting Ready for the Cold

In the fall, it starts getting colder. Animals know that winter is coming. They must prepare. Some animals, like squirrels, begin to collect food. They bury it. They also hide it in trees. They will dig it up later. Other animals, like foxes, begin to grow thick coats of fur. These coats will keep them warm on winter days. Animals also build shelters. Shelters keep them safe and dry. How do you get ready for winter?

Answer the questions below.

1. What do animals begin to collect in the fall?

_____

2. Where do squirrels hide their food?

_____

3. What do foxes grow to get ready for winter?

_____

4. What do animals build to keep safe and dry?

_____

The Star-Spangled Banner

Francis Scott Key wrote a poem called "The Star-Spangled Banner." It honors the American flag. Francis was a lawyer and a poet. He lived in Maryland. In 1812, a war with the British started. Two years later, he saw a fort attacked. In the morning, an American flag was still standing. Francis wrote the poem about it. That poem was made into a song. The song is now the US national anthem.

Circle **yes** or **no**.

1. Francis Scott Key wrote "The Star-Spangled Banner."	Yes	No
2. "The Star-Spangled Banner" honors the Canadian flag.	Yes	No
3. Francis Scott Key was a soldier and a poet.	Yes	No
4. Francis's poem is about Maryland.	Yes	No

A Police Officer's Job

The police protect us. They keep us safe. Police officers go to a special school. They learn how to do their jobs. You may see them walking around. Maybe you see them riding in patrol cars. Sometimes they ride on motorcycles or bicycles. Police officers help when there is an emergency. If you are lost, a police officer can help you. You can spot police officers by their uniforms.

Complete the sentences. Use the words shown.

safe   motorcycle   protect   school

1. A police officer's job is to _____ people.

2. They keep us _____ .

3. Police officers go to a special _____ .

4. Sometimes a police officer rides a _____ .

President Abraham Lincoln

Abraham Lincoln grew up in a log cabin. His family was very poor. He always wanted to help people. This is why he studied hard. Soon, he became a lawyer. People thought he was fair and honest. He believed in freedom for all. Later he became president. He was the tallest president ever. He was also the first president to have a beard. As president, he helped free the slaves. We still honor him today.

Complete the sentences.

1. Abraham Lincoln grew up in a _____ .

2. People thought he was _____ .

3. He was the _____ president ever.

4. He helped free the _____ .

Snowy Day Ice Cream

The snow is falling. There is not a lot to do. Make snow ice cream! It is easy.

Put a big bowl outside. Let it fill with fresh snow.

Scoop the snow into smaller bowls.

Add two spoonfuls of maple syrup to each bowl.

Then add five spoonfuls of heavy cream to each bowl.

Stir it all together.

Eat it before it melts!

What is the order? Draw a line to each step.

First	Stir it all together.
Second	Add two spoonfuls of maple syrup.
Third	Scoop the snow into smaller bowls.
Fourth	Add five spoonfuls of heavy cream.
Last	Put a big bowl outside.

It's for the Birds

It is hard for birds to find food in winter. The ground might be covered in snow. It can be too cold to find seeds and grubs. You can help feed the birds. You can buy birdseed and a bird feeder. Fill the feeder and put it by your window. You can watch the birds eat. Be very quiet. You do not want to scare them. Write down what you see.

Complete the sentences. Use the words shown.

window	birdseed	grubs	snow

1. It is hard for birds to find food in winter because the ground is covered in _____ .

2. It can be too cold to find seeds and _____ .

3. You can buy _____ for birds to eat .

4. To watch them eat, you can put a bird feeder by a _____ .

ARRR Mate!

There's a special holiday for pirates. It is called Talk Like a Pirate Day! It is on September 19. Two men named John and Mark came up with it. They were playing a ball game. One of them shouted, "ARRR"! That gave them the idea. The day celebrates the way pirates used to talk. Anyone can participate. Just talk like a pirate. You can growl, scowl, or say, "ARRR"!

Circle yes or no.

1. Talk Like a Pirate Day is on September 19.	Yes	No
2. Two men named John and Mark came up with the idea.	Yes	No
3. The day celebrates the way pirates used to sail.	Yes	No
4. Only certain people can celebrate.	Yes	No

Thanksgiving

Thanksgiving is a big holiday. It is celebrated in the United States. It is on the fourth Thursday in November. People give thanks for the good in their lives. Many spend the day with friends and family. Some people watch a parade. Others watch football on TV. Most eat a big meal. You may eat turkey and stuffing. People have pumpkin pie too. Yum!

Answer the questions below.

1. When is Thanksgiving celebrated?

_____

2. Why do people celebrate Thanksgiving?

_____

3. What do some people watch on Thanksgiving?

_____

4. What are some foods people eat on Thanksgiving?

_____

An Elephant's Trunk

What animal has the biggest nose? The elephant! Elephants use their trunks for many things. They use it to hug. They can pull a tree out of the ground with their trunk. They even pat their babies with it. They use it to drink. And of course they can sniff with it. They can smell food and water. They can even smell enemies. An elephant's trunk does many things.

Circle **yes** or **no**.

1. An elephant can hug with its trunk.	Yes	No
2. An elephant cannot pull a tree out of the ground.	Yes	No
3. An elephant cannot drink water with its trunk.	Yes	No
4. An elephant can smell enemies with its trunk.	Yes	No

Spinning Webs

Fall is a good time to look for spiderwebs. They might have dew on them. This helps you see them better. Spiders eat insects. Their webs catch them. There are many kinds of spiders. Each builds a different kind of web. The webs are made of silk. Webs are very delicate. They break easily. A spider might build a new web every day.

Circle the correct answers below.

1. What can help you see a spider web?   snow   mud   dew

2. What do spiders eat?

3. What is a spider web made out of?   wool   silk   wire

4. How often can a spider build a new web?   every day   once   never

Pressing Flowers

Let's press flowers! You will need books, tissue paper, and flowers. Pansies, daffodils, and violets are nice flowers to use. Make sure the flowers are not wet. Open the book. Lay down a sheet of tissue paper. Put flowers on it. Cover with another tissue. Then close the book. Pile more books on top of it. Wait a few weeks. The flowers will be dry and flat. You can use them for art projects.

What is the order? Draw a line to each step.

First	Close the book.
Second	Pile more books on top.
Third	Open the book.
Fourth	Put a flower on the tissue.
Last	Lay out the tissue paper.

Alexander Graham Bell

Alexander Graham Bell is credited with inventing the telephone. He was born in a country called Scotland. His mother was deaf. Later, he married a deaf woman. He wanted to learn more about how sound works. Alexander became an inventor. He invented many things. The most famous was the telephone. He made the first phone call to his helper, Mr. Watson. He said, "Mr. Watson, come here. I want to see you." His invention changed the world.

Circle **yes** or **no**.

1. Alexander Graham Bell invented the computer.	Yes	No
2. Alexander Graham Bell married a deaf woman.	Yes	No
3. Alexander Graham Bell wanted to learn how sound works.	Yes	No
4. He made his first phone call to his mother.	Yes	No

A Scientist's Job

Do you like science? Science is the study of the world around us. People who study science are called scientists. Their job is to look for clues about our world. Sometimes they do experiments. This helps them learn how nature works. There are many types of scientists. Some study Earth. Others study space. Some study the weather. There are too many to name! We can learn a lot about our world from scientists.

Circle the correct answers below.

1. What are people who study science called?　　mail carriers　　scientists　　pilots

2. What do scientists look for?　　clues　　water　　food

3. What do scientists do to help them learn?　　lessons　　laundry　　experiments

4. What do some scientists study?

Schools Past and Present

Today, most kids go to school in a building. The school might have a lot of rooms. Each class has a teacher. In each class, kids are about the same age. Hundreds of years ago, schools were different. There was only one room. Kids of all ages sat together. One teacher taught them all. In the future, schools might change again.

Circle **yes** or **no**.

1. Today, there is one teacher for all the grades.	Yes	No
2. Today, schools might have a lot of rooms.	Yes	No
3. Hundreds of years ago, children went to school in one room.	Yes	No
4. In the past, kids of all ages sat together.	Yes	No

Let's Look at Soil

Soil is usually brown. It looks like dirt. But it is much more. It is made up of many things. It is made up of rocks. It is also made up of living and dead life forms. Soil also has minerals. Soil helps plants grow. It is food for plants. The top layer has nutrients. These nutrients keep plants healthy. This is the layer that we can see. It has taken millions of years for Earth's soil to be what it is today.

Complete the sentences. Use the words shown.

healthy	nutrients	rocks	plants

1. One thing that makes up soil is _____ .

2. Soil is food for _____ .

3. The top layer has _____ .

4. Nutrients keep plants _____ .

A-CHOO!

Sneezing is funny. You feel a tickle in your nose. Dust or mold could be the problem. It could be pollen from flowers. Your nose sends a message to your sneeze center. This is a part of your brain. The sneeze center helps you sneeze. Muscles in your body work together. Your eyes close. Your lungs push out air. Your stomach tightens. This all helps to form a sneeze. Sneezing gets rid of the tickle. You can thank the sneeze center!

Circle the correct answers below.

1. What might you feel in your nose before a sneeze?   tickle   pencil   paper

2. What does the sneeze center make you do?   eat   sleep   sneeze

3. What could make you sneeze?

4. What must work together to form a sneeze?   friends   toes   muscles

Eleanor Roosevelt

Eleanor Roosevelt was a First Lady of the United States. She married President Franklin D. Roosevelt. Eleanor grew up in New York. She had a hard childhood. Her parents died when she was a kid. As first lady she helped others. She talked to people all over the country. Then she told her husband how to help. She also met with soldiers hurt at war. Today we honor her. We remember her work.

Answer the questions.

1. Who was Eleanor Roosevelt?

_____

2. Where did Eleanor Roosevelt grow up?

_____

3. Whom did Eleanor Roosevelt marry?

_____

4. Whom did she meet with when they were hurt?

_____

Buzz, Buzz, Buzz

Honeybees live in hives. Honeybees make honey. Bees work together. Each bee has a job. The queen bee lays eggs. Some worker bees build the honeycomb. Others take care of the larvae. The larvae are the baby bees. Others collect food. These bees fly from flower to flower. They gather nectar and pollen. They store it in their throats. Then they turn it into honey. Bees work very hard.

Circle the correct answers below.

1. Where do honeybees live?	hives	stones	flowers
2. What is the job of the queen bee?	to eat	to lay eggs	to sing
3. What do some worker bees collect for the hive?	flowers	food	sticks
4. Where do the bees store nectar and pollen?	their feet	their wings	their throats

Air Pollution

Air pollution is when the air is dirty. This can come from gases or dust. It can also come from bad smells. Cars and factories cause air pollution. Air pollution is not good for our bodies. It can be harmful. We cannot see air pollution. Don't worry! There are many things we can do to stop it. We can ride a bike instead of driving. We can turn off lights when we are not using them. We can also recycle.

Complete the sentences.

1. Air pollution is caused by _____ .

2. Air pollution is bad for our _____ .

3. To fight air pollution, we can ride a _____ .

4. We can also turn off the _____ in our house.

Tasting Food

Go to a mirror. Stick out your tongue. Can you see tiny bumps? These are taste buds. You have about 10,000 taste buds! They help you taste food. Some foods are salty. Some are sweet. Others are sour or bitter. Taste buds help you taste these flavors. How do they do it? Taste buds have tiny hairs. These tiny hairs send messages to your brain. They say that apples are sweet or that chips are salty. Taste buds help us enjoy food.

Circle the correct answers below.

1. Where are your taste buds?			
2. What do taste buds help you do?	read	taste	sleep
3. How many taste buds do you have?	50	10,000	100
4. How big are taste buds?	big	giant	tiny

All About Plants

A flower is part of a plant. Flowers come in different colors and shapes. Plants also have other parts. They have roots. The roots feed the plant. They have leaves. Leaves help make food from sunlight. They also have a stem. The stem brings water to the leaves. Some plants even have fruit. Each part of the plant has a job. Flowers attract bees. When you see a plant, look for all its parts.

Circle **yes** or **no**.

1. Flowers come in only one shape.	Yes	No
2. Plants have only one part.	Yes	No
3. The roots attract bees.	Yes	No
4. The stem brings water to the leaves.	Yes	No

Table of Contents

Most books have a table of contents. It is in the beginning of the book. It is a list of parts in a book. Look at the table of contents below.

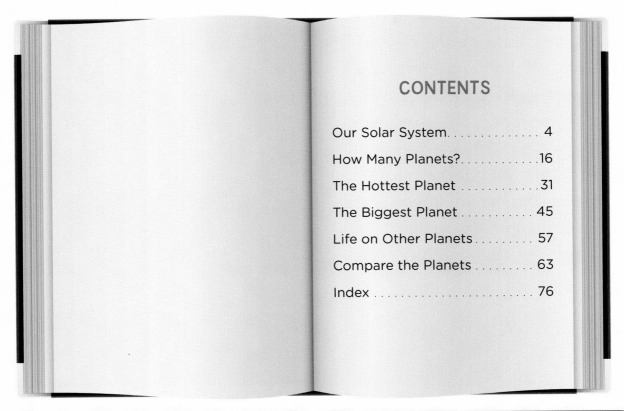

CONTENTS

Answer the questions.

1. What is this book about?

_____

2. On what page would you find information on the hottest planet?

_____

3. On what page would you find information on the biggest planet?

_____

4. On what page would you find information comparing the planets' rings?

_____

Veterans Day

Veterans Day is a day to honor veterans. A veteran is a person who served in the armed forces. We celebrate this day on November 11. Schools are closed. Some workplaces are closed. There are many parades. Veterans march in the parades. The president gives a speech. He talks about how brave our soldiers are. If you see veterans you can thank them. They help keep our country safe.

Circle the correct answers below.

1. Whom does Veterans Day honor?

2. During what month do we celebrate Veterans Day?   May   November   June

3. With what do we celebrate on this day?   sleep   parades   cars

4. What does the president give on this day?   a job   a speech   a gift

Germs

Our bodies are strong. They work hard to stay healthy. Sometimes we get sick. This happens when bad germs get into our bodies. Germs are tiny. They are alive. We can't see them with our eyes. We can only see them with a tool. This tool is called a microscope. Germs are found around the world. They attack people, plants, and animals. How can you stay germfree? Wash your hands often!

Answer the questions below.

1. What happens when germs get into our bodies?

_____

2. How would you describe germs?

_____

3. How can we see germs?

_____

4. How can we protect ourselves from germs?

_____

Call the Tooth Fairy!

Have you lost any teeth yet? Your baby teeth will all fall out. They fall out for good reason. They make room for your big teeth. Big teeth are under your gums. They push your baby teeth out. Then they have room to grow. You will have all of your big teeth when you are 12 or 13. You will have 28 of them. When you are a grown-up, you might get four more! That's 32 teeth!

Circle **yes** or **no**.

1. Baby teeth fall out to make room for big teeth.	Yes	No
2. Big teeth are under your gums.	Yes	No
3. You will have all your big teeth when you are 8.	Yes	No
4. Some grown-ups have 32 teeth.	Yes	No

Honor Our Presidents

Presidents Day is the same day every year. It is the third Monday in February. The holiday honors US presidents. This day was chosen with care. It is close to George Washington's birthday. He was the first US president. The holiday is also close to Abraham Lincoln's birthday. He was the 16th president. Some states honor other presidents. School is closed on Presidents Day!

Complete the sentences.

1. Presidents Day honors _____ .

2. It is on the _____ Monday in February.

3. Some states honor _____ presidents.

4. School is _____ on Presidents Day.

Making Applesauce

Applesauce is a yummy snack. It is easy to make. Just make sure you have a grown-up help you.

You will need:

2 apples

1 tablespoon lemon juice

2 teaspoons sugar

2 pinches cinnamon

A blender

A bowl

Peel the apples. Chop them up. Throw away the core. Blend apples and lemon juice in a blender. Pour the mixture into a bowl. Add the sugar and the cinnamon. Mix. Enjoy!

What is the order? Draw a line to each step.

First	Add sugar and cinnamon.
Second	Pour into a bowl.
Third	Peel the apples.
Fourth	Chop the apples.
Last	Blend apples and lemon juice.

Equal Rights

Martin Luther King Jr. was an important man. He fought for equal rights. He wanted people of all colors to have the same rights. He was so smart he skipped two grades in school. Martin Luther King Jr. made many speeches. One speech was called "I Have a Dream." Many people heard this speech. He hoped for new laws. Many people liked what he said. Some did not. Soon new laws were passed. These laws were called civil rights.

Circle the correct answers below.

1. What did Martin Luther King Jr. talk about?   equal rights   school   cars

2. How many grades did Martin Luther King Jr. skip in school?   four   two   one

3. What was Martin Luther King Jr. famous for?   running   speeches   cooking

4. What were the new laws called?

    civil rights   people's rights   kid's rights

What Are Scars?

Have you ever scraped your knee? Have you ever fallen off a bike? Have you ever bled? Sometimes we get cuts. A big cut may leave a scar. A scar is a patch of skin. It grows after a cut. It's the body's way of healing the skin. Most people have scars. Some people have scars from operations. Warriors from long ago used to show off their scars. They would tell stories about how they got the scar. What's your scar story?

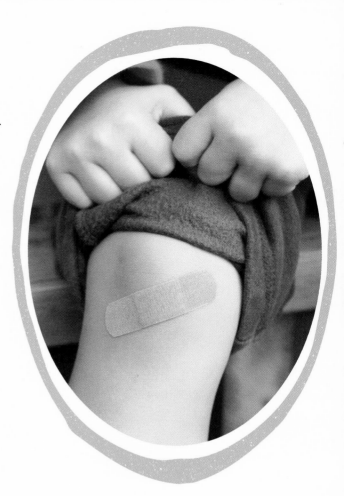

Answer the questions below.

1. What is a scar?

_____

2. When can it grow?

_____

3. What does a scar help heal?

_____

4. Why do you think warriors would show off their scars?

_____

Why We Need Sleep

Sleep is healthy. Sleep feels good. We need sleep. It helps our bodies rest. Not sleeping enough makes us cranky. When you sleep, your brain is working. It uses sleep time to solve problems. It also sorts the things you learned that day. Most kids sleep 10 hours a night. It is important to get lots of sleep. It helps you be ready for the next day.

Circle the correct answers below.

1. What does sleep help your body do?	fly	eat	rest
2. What might you get if you don't have enough sleep?	cranky	happy	hungry
3. What does your brain solve while you are sleeping?	problems	puzzles	math
4. How many hours do most kids sleep?	20	2	10

The Fourth of July!

July 4 is called Independence Day. It is a fun summer holiday. It is the day the Declaration of Independence was signed. This meant that the United States was free from the British. The British used to rule the United States. Today, people celebrate on this day. Many businesses are closed. There are parades. People have parties with friends and family. At night there are fireworks. It's a fun holiday!

Circle yes or no.

1. The Fourth of July is in the winter.	Yes	No
2. It is called Independence Day because businesses are closed.	Yes	No
3. The British used to rule the United States.	Yes	No
4. Everybody goes to work on Independence Day.	Yes	No

Food for Fuel

Your body is like a car. It needs fuel. You get fuel from healthy food. Healthy food helps your body run. Breakfast is an important meal. You have not had fuel all night. Your body needs to recharge. So sit down and eat a good meal. You can get fuel from fruits. Vegetables are very healthy. Grains and protein are also good. They will help you get all the fuel you need. What's your favorite breakfast?

Answer the questions below. Use the words shown.

fuel	breakfast	healthy	recharge

1. What does your body need to run? _____

2. What is an important meal to eat? _____

3. What does your body need to do in the morning? _____

4. What kind of food helps your body run? _____

The Crack in the Bell

The Liberty Bell is a big bell. It is located in Philadelphia. It is a symbol of freedom. People rang the bell at important times. The bell has a huge crack in it. It was being tested when it cracked. A new bell was made. It cracked too! The crack changed the sound of the bell. This time the crack stayed. It is still there today.

Circle **yes** or **no**.

1. People rang the bell at important times.	Yes	No
2. A new bell was made.	Yes	No
3. The crack did not change the sound.	Yes	No
4. The crack is not there now.	Yes	No

Ocean Tides

The ocean is fun. It's great for swimming. It's best to swim near the shore. The shore is where the ocean meets the land. This is where the tides come in. Tides are swells of water. Tides change how deep the water is. High tides can cover the beach. The water is deep. Low tide is when the tides go out. The water is not as deep. We can see more of the sandy beach at low tide.

Complete the sentences.

1. The shore is where the ocean meets the _____ .

2. Tides are _____ of water.

3. The tides change how _____ the water is.

4. We can see more of the sandy beach at _____ tide.

A Symbol of Strength

Have you ever seen a bald eagle? They are hard to find. They are a symbol of our country. They stand for strength. They also stand for bravery. The bald eagle is a powerful bird. Our Founding Fathers chose this symbol. Some did not want the eagle. Benjamin Franklin did not. He said he would prefer the turkey! You can find the eagle on the United States seal.

Answer the questions below.

1. What does the bald eagle stand for?

_____

2. Who chose the eagle?

_____

3. What would Benjamin Franklin have picked over the bald eagle?

_____

4. Where can you find the symbol of the bald eagle?

_____